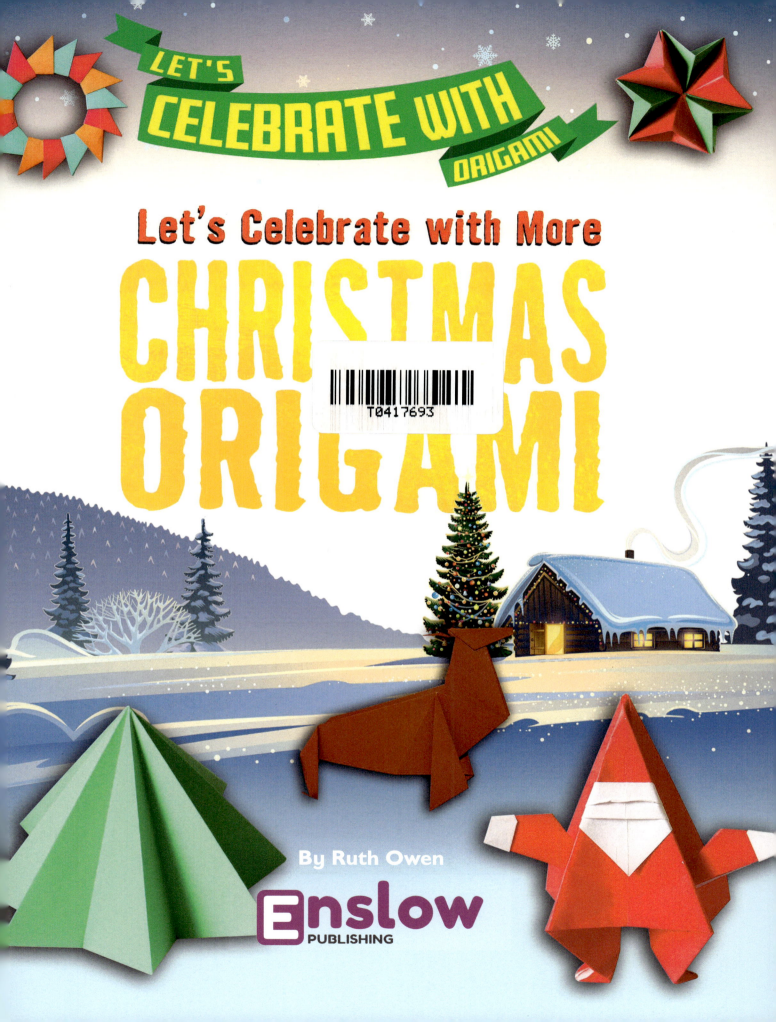

LET'S CELEBRATE WITH ORIGAMI

Let's Celebrate with More
CHRISTMAS ORIGAMI

By Ruth Owen

Enslow
PUBLISHING

Published in 2022 by Enslow Publishing, LLC
29 East 21st Street
New York, NY 10010

Produced for Rosen by Ruth Owen Books
Designer: Emma Randall
Photos courtesy of Ruth Owen Books and Shutterstock

Cataloging-in-Publication Data

Names: Owen, Ruth.
Title: Let's celebrate with more Christmas origami / Ruth Owen.
Description: New York : Enslow Publishing, 2022. | Series: Let's celebrate with origami | Includes glossary and index.
Identifiers: ISBN 9781978526556 (pbk.) | ISBN 9781978526570 (library bound) | ISBN 9781978526563 (6 pack) | ISBN 9781978526587 (ebook)
Subjects: LCSH: Origami--Juvenile literature. | Christmas decorations--Juvenile literature.
Classification: LCC TT870.O946 2022 | DDC 736'.982--dc23

Manufactured in the United States of America

CPSIA compliance information: Batch #CWENS22: For further information contact Enslow Publishing, New York, New York at 1-800-398-2504

Find us on

Contents

Happy Holidays... 4

Origami Tips 6

Paper Angels 8

Star of Bethlehem 12

Fold a Christmas Tree...................................... 16

Let's Make Santa... 20

A Flying Reindeer.. 24

A Colorful Wreath 28

Glossary, Index, Websites 32

Happy Holidays

Did you know that just by folding paper you can make Christmas decorations and **unique** gifts? If you love crafting for your friends and family, you will love **origami**.

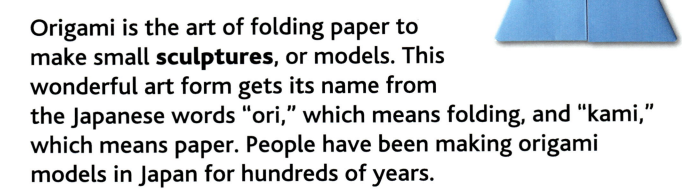

Origami is the art of folding paper to make small **sculptures**, or models. This wonderful art form gets its name from the Japanese words "ori," which means folding, and "kami," which means paper. People have been making origami models in Japan for hundreds of years.

If you've never tried origami before, don't be nervous! This book will show you how to make mini Christmas trees, stars, a paper Santa, a wreath, angels, and even a reindeer. So get some paper and let's get folding!

Origami Tips

Follow these tips for successful folding and origami model making.

Tip 1

Read all the instructions carefully and look at the pictures. Make sure you understand what's required before you begin a fold. Don't rush; be patient. Work slowly and carefully.

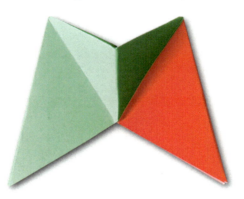

Tip 2

Folding a piece of paper sounds easy, but it can be tricky to get neat, accurate folds. The more you practice, the easier it becomes.

Tip 3

If an instruction says "crease," make the crease as flat as possible. The flatter the creases, the better the model. You can make a sharp crease by running a plastic ruler along the edge of the paper.

Tip 4

Sometimes, at first, your models may look a little crumpled. Don't give up! The more models you make, the better you will get at folding and creasing.

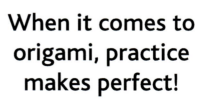

When it comes to origami, practice makes perfect!

The amazing Christmas tree and star models on this page were made by an experienced origami model maker. Keep practicing and you could soon be making complicated models like these!

Some of the origami models in this book can be used to create homemade Christmas cards. Try gluing Santa or some angels to a piece of cardboard. Add a bow and you will have a very special and personal Christmas greeting.

Paper Angels

In the Christmas story, an angel named Gabriel appeared to Mary. The angel told Mary she would give birth to Jesus, the son of God. When Jesus was born in a stable in Bethlehem, an angel appeared to shepherds who were tending their sheep nearby. The angel announced to the shepherds that a savior had been born.

Angels are an important part of the Christmas story and have become a much-loved holiday decoration. They are even placed on the top of many Christmas trees.

These origami angels are very simple to make. You will quickly be able to create a host of beautiful paper angels to decorate your home.

To make origami angels, you will need:

Sheets of origami paper in colors of your choice

(Origami paper is sometimes colored on both sides or white on one side.)

Scissors

STEP 1:

Place the paper colored side down. Fold in half from side to side, crease, and unfold. Then fold down from top to bottom, crease, and unfold.

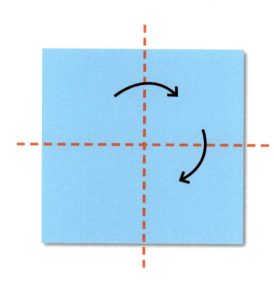

STEP 2:

Turn the paper over. Fold in half from side to side, crease, and unfold. Then fold down from top to bottom, crease, and unfold.

STEP 3:

Place the paper colored side down. Using the creases you've just made, collapse and fold up the paper to form a flattened triangle by bringing A in to meet B, point C down to meet point D, and point E down to meet point F.

As you collapse and fold up the paper, it should look like this.

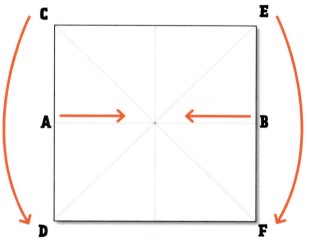

flattened triangle

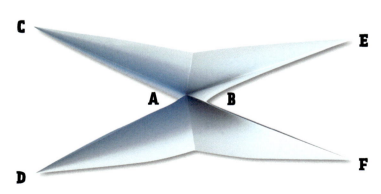

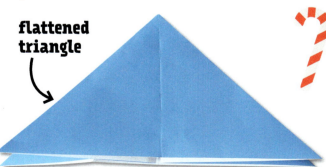

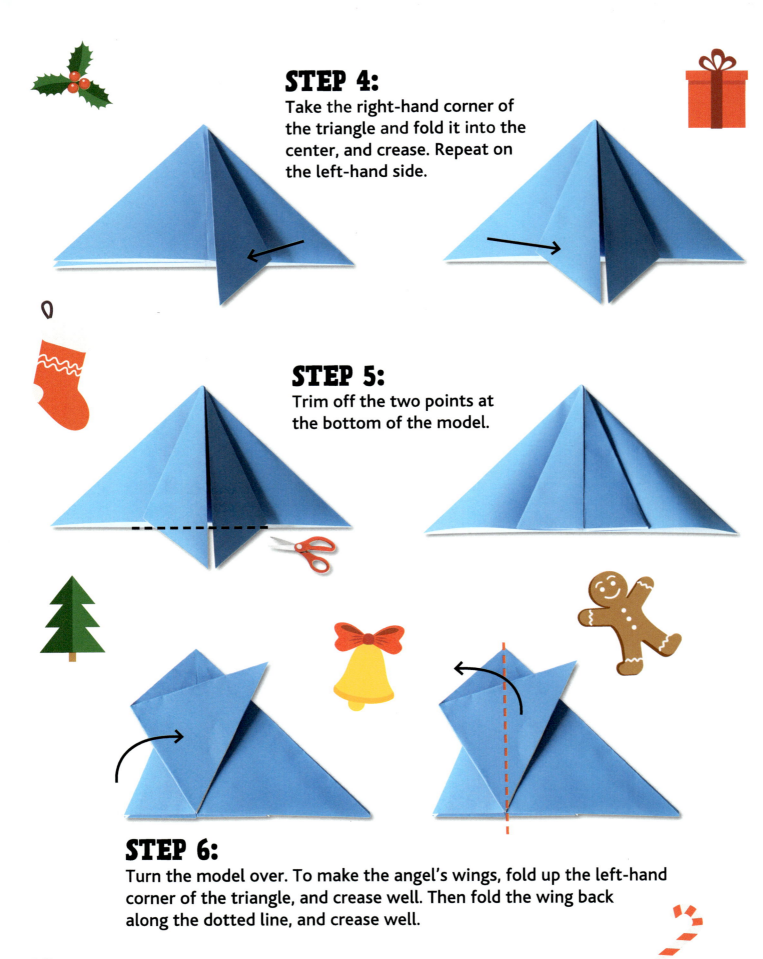

STEP 4:
Take the right-hand corner of the triangle and fold it into the center, and crease. Repeat on the left-hand side.

STEP 5:
Trim off the two points at the bottom of the model.

STEP 6:
Turn the model over. To make the angel's wings, fold up the left-hand corner of the triangle, and crease well. Then fold the wing back along the dotted line, and crease well.

STEP 7:

Repeat on the right-hand side. Your model should now look like this.

STEP 8:

Turn the model over. Fold in points A and B along the dotted lines to make the angel's hands.

A

B

Your origami angel is complete. Gently open out the bottom of the model to help it stand.

Star of Bethlehem

In this project, you will learn how to create a six-pointed Christmas star. Stars are a very special Christmas **symbol**. Do you know why?

In the Christmas story, a bright star appears in the sky when Jesus is born. The star leads the three wise men to Bethlehem to the birthplace of Jesus. The star is sometimes called the Star of Bethlehem.

You can use origami paper or scraps of Christmas gift-wrapping paper to make your model. You can even use your star model as a decoration for the top of your Christmas tree.

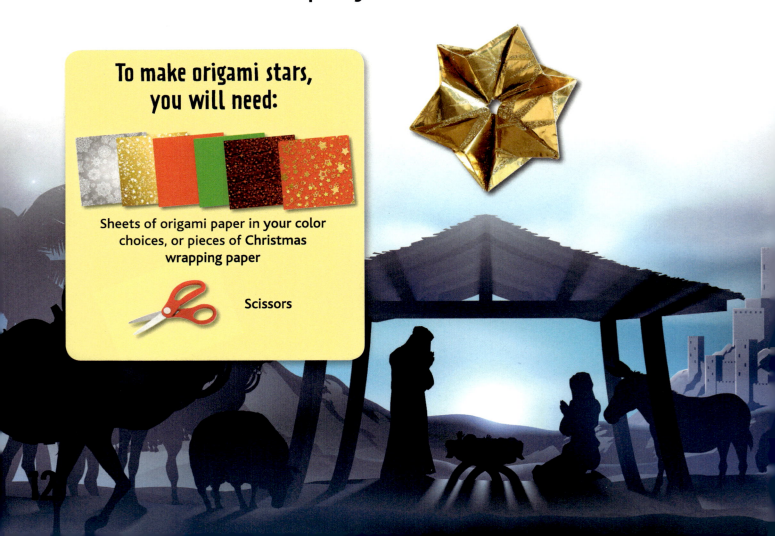

To make origami stars, you will need:

Sheets of origami paper in your color choices, or pieces of Christmas wrapping paper

Scissors

STEP 1:

To make a star that's approximately 3 inches (8 cm) across, you will need six small squares of paper that are 3 inches (8 cm) square.

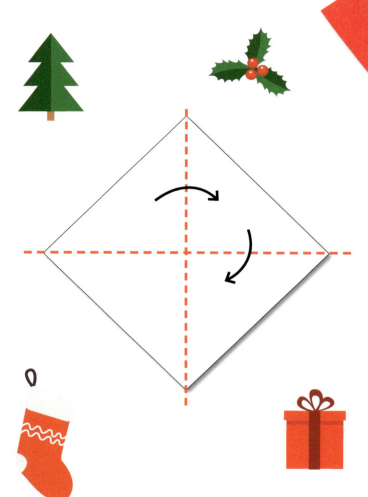

STEP 2:

Take one square of paper. Place it colored side down. Fold in half from one side to the other, crease, and unfold. Then fold down from top to bottom, crease, and unfold.

STEP 3:

Turn the paper over. Fold in half from side to side, crease, and unfold. Then fold down from top to bottom, crease, and unfold.

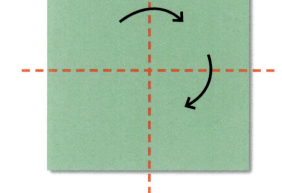

STEP 4:

Place the paper colored side down. Using the creases you've just made, collapse and fold up the paper to form a flattened triangle by bringing A in to meet B, point C down to meet point D, and point E down to meet point F.

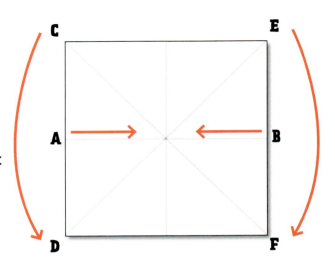

As you collapse and fold up the paper, it should look like this.

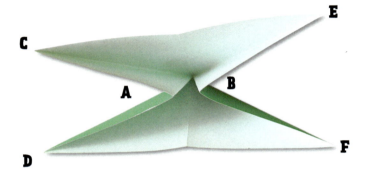

flattened triangle

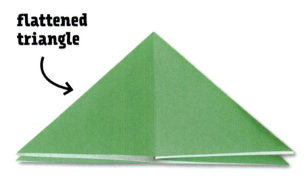

STEP 5:

Repeat steps 2 to 4 with the other five squares of paper.

STEP 6:

Now take two triangles and gently slide the points of one triangle inside the points of the other, so that the two triangles slot together tightly.

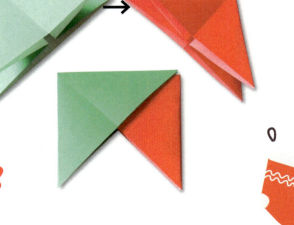

STEP 7:

At the top of your model, there will be a pocket. Gently squeeze the two triangles together so that the pocket pops open. Keep gently squeezing and opening out the pocket, creasing as you go, so it becomes beak-like.

pocket

beak-like pocket

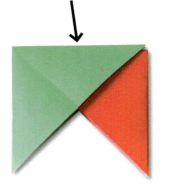
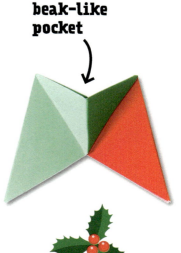

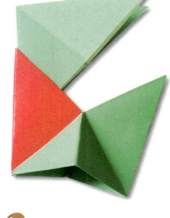

STEP 8:

Now repeat steps 6 and 7 with a third triangle.

Beak-like pocket

STEP 9:

Keep slotting the triangles together. Open out each of the pockets on the edges of the model, squeezing and creasing them to form beak-like pockets.

beak-like pockets

STEP 10:

Once all six triangles are slotted together, complete the star by slotting the points of triangle six into triangle one. This is tricky, so work slowly and be patient!

Fold a Christmas Tree

When twinkly, decorated Christmas trees start to appear, we know that Christmas is on the way! This year, try making some mini origami trees to use as decorations and to give as gifts.

These tiny trees are perfect as a table decoration. You can also give them to the adults you know who work in offices to brighten up their desks during the holiday season.

The origami trees also squash flat, so you can pop them inside your Christmas cards and send everyone you know their own origami tree.

To make origami Christmas trees, you will need:

Sheets of origami paper in shades of green

STEP 1:

Place the paper white side down. Fold in half from side to side, crease, and unfold. Then fold down from top to bottom, crease, and unfold.

STEP 2:

Turn the paper over. Fold in half from side to side, crease, and unfold. Then fold down from top to bottom, crease, and unfold.

STEP 3:

Using the creases you've just made, collapse and fold up the paper to form a flattened diamond shape by bringing A in to meet B, and point C down to meet point D.

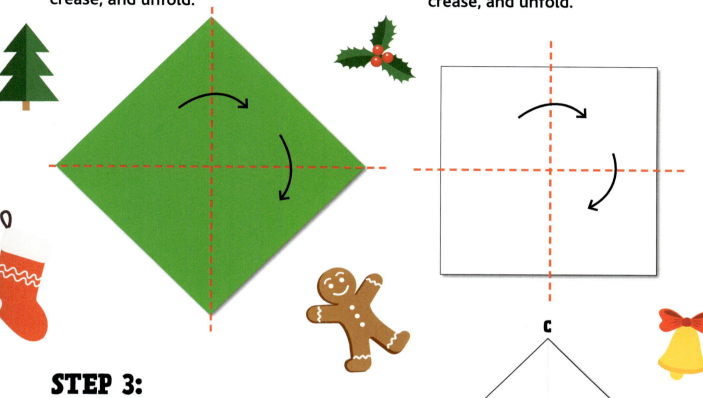

As you collapse and fold up the paper, it should look like this.

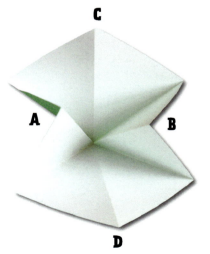

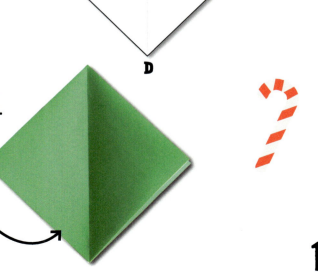

flattened diamond shape

STEP 4:

Fold the right-hand point of the diamond into the center of the model, and crease well. (You are only folding the top layer of paper.)

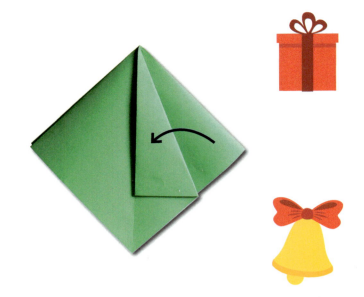

STEP 5:

Gently open out the flap you've just created to form an upside-down kite shape. Squash the flap flat against the model.

flap

STEP 6:

Now repeat steps 4 and 5 on the remaining three side points until your model looks like this.

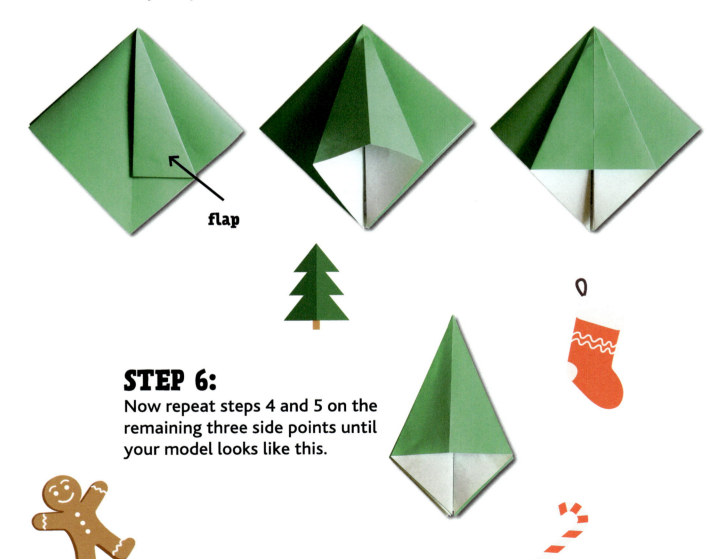

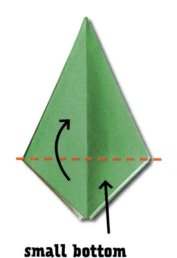

STEP 7:

Rearrange the flaps of your model so it looks like this.

Fold up the bottom of the model along the dotted line, crease hard, and then unfold.

small bottom triangle

The base of the model will now look like this.

STEP 8:

Next, slightly open out your model, and fold each of the small bottom triangles under and inside the model.

STEP 9:

Finally, stand your tree on a flat surface and arrange the creased edges to get an even, rounded shape.

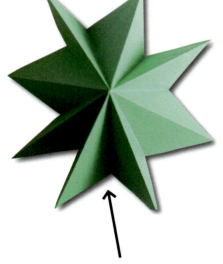

your tree seen from above

Let's Make Santa

This fantastic origami Santa is a complicated model with lots of steps. But it wouldn't be Christmas without the jolly fellow in the red suit. If you follow the directions closely and work slowly and carefully, your very own origami Santa will soon appear from just a single sheet of red paper.

To make an origami Santa, you will need:

One sheet of origami paper that's red on one side and white on the other

STEP 1:
Place the paper white side down. Fold the paper in half from side to side, crease, and unfold. Next, fold down from top to bottom, crease, and unfold.

STEP 2:
Fold each side point into the center crease of the model, and crease well.

STEP 3:
Fold the two points back along the dotted lines, and crease.

STEP 4:
Now unfold all the creases you've just made and flatten the paper.

STEP 5:
To make Santa's hands, fold in the two side points of the paper, and crease. Only fold in the points about 1/5 inch (0.5 cm). Then fold each point over again by 1/5 inch (0.5 cm).

STEP 6:
Now fold the paper in half along the dotted line, and crease well.

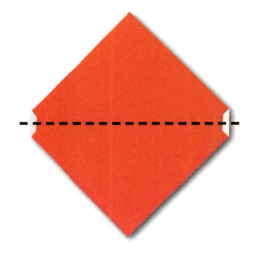

STEP 7:
Now fold up the bottom point of the model to meet the top edge of the model, and crease well.

STEP 8:

Next, working only with the top layer of paper, fold down the center point to make Santa's face and beard.

Then fold down point A so that a thin edge of the beard can still be seen.

Now fold point A back up along the dotted line and fold it behind itself to create a straight edge.

straight edge

top edge

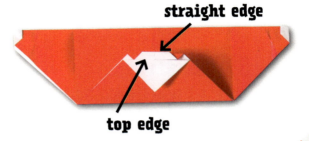

Your model should look like this.

Finally, fold over the top edge of the face to create a furry brim for Santa's cap.

STEP 9:

Fold up the right-hand side of the model along the dotted line, and crease hard. Then unfold. Repeat on the left-hand side of the model.

STEP 10:

Now fold in the two sides of the model along the dotted lines, and crease hard. Then unfold.

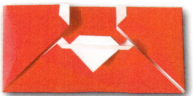

STEP 11:

Next, fold down the two sides of the model, and crease hard.

STEP 12:

Take hold of the hand on the right-hand side of the model and open out the folds you made in steps 9 to 11. Then using the folds marked with the dotted lines, flatten the right-hand side against the model.

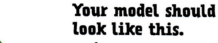

Your model should look like this.

Now repeat on the left-hand side of the model.

STEP 13:

Fold in both sides of the model and crease hard. Your model should now form a triangle with Santa's face in the center.

STEP 14:

Fold the right-hand side of the model backward along the dotted line, and crease hard. Repeat on the left-hand side.

STEP 15:

Gently pull and fold out Santa's arms from inside the body.

brim of cap

STEP 16:

Crumple the brim of Santa's cap to make it look like fur. Finally, make Santa's feet by folding up the bottom of each leg. Your origami Santa is complete!

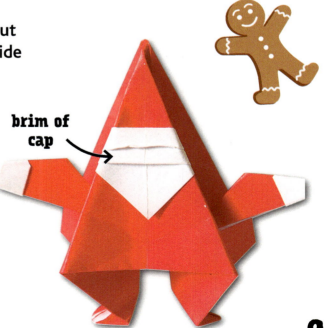

A Flying Reindeer

In Christmas stories, reindeer have glossy, reddish-brown coats and can sometimes even fly! In real life, however, these deer, which live in the **Arctic** region, have thick coats of white and brownish-gray hair—and they definitely can't fly!

Stories say that on Christmas Eve, when Santa sets off from the North Pole to deliver gifts around the world, his sleigh is pulled by a team of eight flying reindeer. These magical reindeer are named Dasher, Dancer, Prancer, Vixen, Comet, Cupid, Donner, and Blitzen.

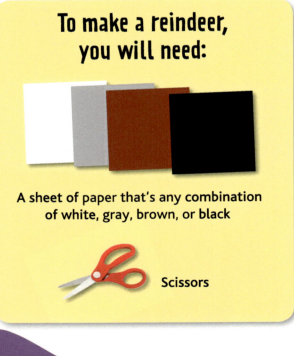

To make a reindeer, you will need:

A sheet of paper that's any combination of white, gray, brown, or black

Scissors

STEP 1:

Place the paper brown side down. Fold in half, and then unfold. (Our paper was brown on one side and black on the other.)

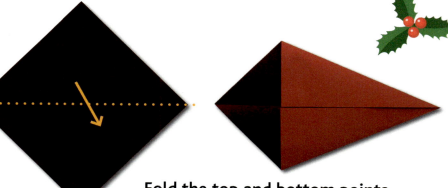

Fold the top and bottom points into the center crease to make a kite shape, and crease well.

STEP 2:

Now fold the top and bottom points on the left-hand side into the center crease, and crease well.

STEP 3:

Turn the model 90 degrees clockwise. Then fold up the bottom point of the model to meet the top point, crease, and then unfold.

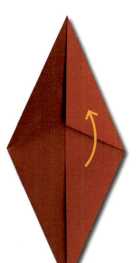

STEP 4:

Open out the top right-hand triangle to create a pocket. Using the creases you've previously made, gently squash and flatten the pocket to make a point.

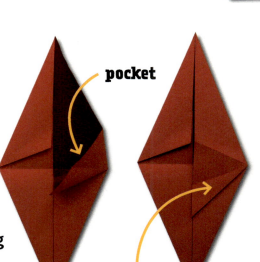

pocket

flattened point

Then repeat on the left-hand side.

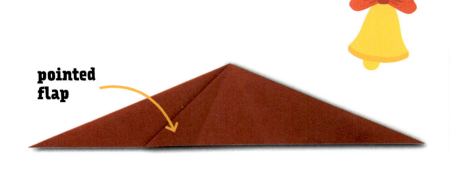

STEP 5:

Turn the model 90 degrees clockwise and then fold in half along the center crease. Make sure you have a flap of paper pointing toward the left-hand side of the model.

pointed flap

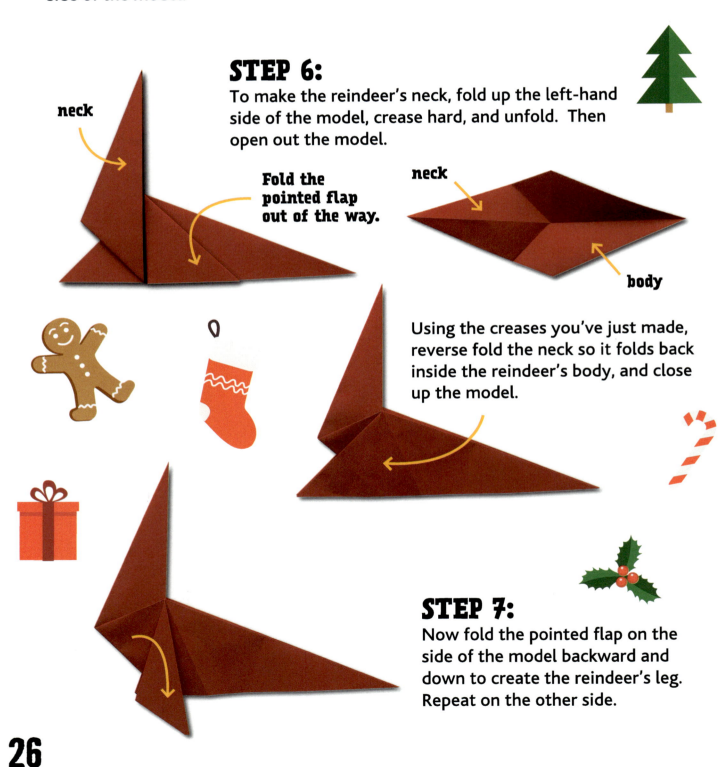

neck

STEP 6:

To make the reindeer's neck, fold up the left-hand side of the model, crease hard, and unfold. Then open out the model.

Fold the pointed flap out of the way.

neck

body

Using the creases you've just made, reverse fold the neck so it folds back inside the reindeer's body, and close up the model.

STEP 7:

Now fold the pointed flap on the side of the model backward and down to create the reindeer's leg. Repeat on the other side.

STEP 8:

To make the reindeer's head, fold down the top of the neck, crease hard, and unfold. Open out and flatten the head section. Fold the tip of the head under, then fold down each side of the head around the neck.

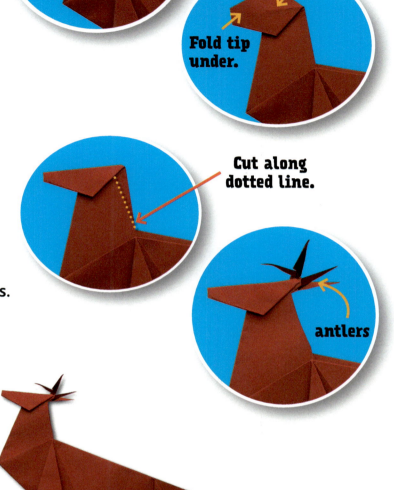

Fold down to enclose the neck.

Fold tip under.

STEP 9:

To make the reindeer's antlers, cut up along the dotted line to the fold of the head. Carefully fold up the sliver of paper you've just cut. Gently separate out the layers of paper in the sliver to make the antlers.

Cut along dotted line.

antlers

STEP 10:

Finally, make a cut up the center of the model on the right-hand side to create two points. Fold down each point to make a leg. Then fold out the tip of each leg to make a foot. You're all done!

two points

A Colorful Wreath

In this final project, you can make an origami paper wreath to hang on a door. You can use origami paper or colorful, sparkling Christmas wrapping paper. You can even make mini wreaths that can be hung on a Christmas tree.

Wreaths are one of the most popular decorations at Christmas. They are often made from natural materials, such as holly, evergreen branches, berries, and flowers. We see them hung on the front doors of houses and outside stores and offices, too.

To make an origami wreath, you will need:

Paper in your choice of colors

A ruler and scissors

Ribbon for hanging

A glue stick

STEP 1:

To make a wreath that measures 7 inches (18 cm) across, you will need 15 pieces of paper each measuring 6 inches by 4 inches (15 cm x 10 cm).

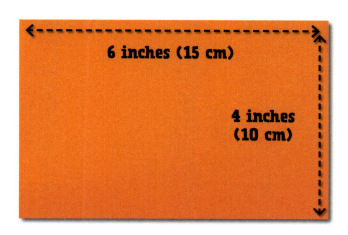

6 inches (15 cm)

4 inches (10 cm)

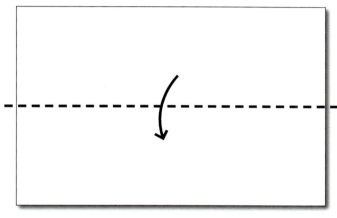

STEP 2:

To make one module of the wreath, place a piece of paper colored side down, fold it in half along the dotted line, and crease hard. Now fold the model in half again along the dotted line, crease, and then unfold.

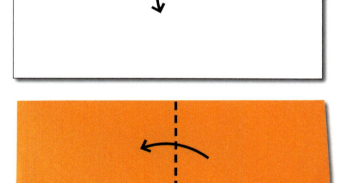

STEP 3:

Fold down the right-hand side of the model to meet the center crease you've just made, and crease hard. Then repeat on the left-hand side.

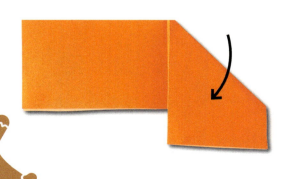

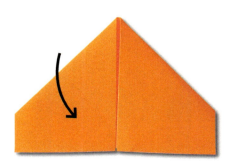

STEP 4:

Turn the model over. Fold up the two bottom corners, and crease.

STEP 5:

Fold up the two flaps at the bottom of the model, and crease. You should now have a triangle.

STEP 6:

Fold the triangle in half. On the left-hand edge of the model, you will now have two pockets. On the lower right-hand side, you will have two points. This is one module of the wreath.

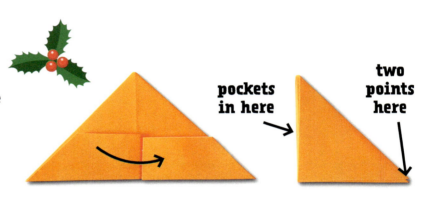

pockets in here

two points here

STEP 7:

Repeat steps 2 to 6 to make 14 more modules, or triangles.

STEP 8:

To begin constructing the wreath, slot the two points of one triangle into the two pockets of another triangle.

STEP 9:
Continue slotting the triangles together.

STEP 10:
Finally, when all the triangles are slotted together, slide the two points of triangle 15 into the pockets of triangle 1 to complete the "circle."

You may want to adjust the positions of the triangles to get them equally spaced and to make the wreath as circular as possible. It's best to do this with the wreath laying on a flat surface. Once you're happy with the wreath's shape, use a glue stick to glue the modules together. Add a ribbon, and your wreath will be ready to hang.

Use tiny rectangles of paper to make a miniwreath that can be hung on a Christmas tree.

Glossary

Arctic
The northernmost area on Earth, which includes northern parts of Europe, Asia, and North America, the Arctic Ocean, the polar ice cap, and the North Pole.

origami
The art of folding paper into decorative shapes or objects.

sculptures
Works of art that have a shape to them, such as statues or carved objects, and may be made of wood, stone, metal, plaster, or even paper.

symbol
Something that stands for or represents another thing, such as an important event or person. For example, a cross may be a symbol of Christianity.

unique
One of a kind.

Index

A
angel origami model, 8–9, 10–11
angels, 4, 7, 8
Arctic, 24

B
Bethlehem, 8, 12

C
Christmas tree origami model, 16–17, 18–19
Christmas trees, 4, 7, 8, 12, 16

G
Gabriel (angel), 8

J
Japan, 4
Jesus, 8, 12

M
Mary, 8

O
origami (general), 4, 6–7

R
reindeer, 4, 24
reindeer origami model, 24–25, 26–27

S
Santa Claus, 4, 7, 20, 24
Santa origami model, 20–21, 22–23
Star of Bethlehem model, 12–13, 14–15
stars, 4, 7, 12

W
wreath origami model, 28–29, 30–31
wreaths, 4, 28

Websites

www.easypeasyandfun.com/christmas-origami-kids/
www.easypeasyandfun.com/christmas-ornaments-for-kids-to-make/
www.origami-fun.com/christmas-origami.html

32

Publisher's note to educators and parents: Our editors have carefully reviewed these websites to ensure that they are suitable for students. Many websites change frequently, however, and we cannot guarantee that a site's future contents will continue to meet our high standards of quality and educational value. Be advised that students should be closely supervised whenever they access the internet.